P9-DEW-602

The Denver Mint

The Story of the Mint
from
the Gold Rush to Today

by   David J. Eitemiller

ACKNOWLEDGEMENTS

It has only been with the help of many people that this book has come into being.

Without the participation and help of the Denver Mint, this book would not have been possible. Ms. Nora Hussey, Superintendent of the Denver Mint, and her assistant, Tito Rael, have given valuable time to provide information on facts and figures concerning the present day operation. They have also proofed the manuscript. Photographs of the interior of the Mint were done by George Basques.

Much of the historical research was done at the Denver Public Library, Western History Department. I am indebted to Ms. Eleanor Gehres and her staff, in particular A. D. Mastrogiuseppe, who aided in picture acquisition. Don Dilley also helped with resources.

Pictures of coins from Clark, Gruber & Co. were provided by the library at the Colorado Heritage Center. Collette Chambellan worked on that, and Mike Butler at the book store helped with back issues of the Colorado Magazine.

Pictures of Clark, Gruber & Co. were provided by Malcom Collier from the Collier Collection of First Federal Savings Bank of Colorado.

Richard Grant at the Denver and Colorado Convention and Visitors Bureau provided several very fine photographs of Denver and the Mint.

The hardest part of writing a book is putting words on paper so that the story flows and is interesting. After writing and re-writing it several times, I became so familiar with it that I didn't know how it sounded. Several people took time to read the manuscript and each one had valuable comments. For their time and trouble, I am grateful to Bill Kotch and Paul Scott in Dallas, and David and Nodeen Reinecke in Denver.

I am deeply grateful to Lola and Leon Enge for painstakingly teaching me about layout and design, as well as how to write a book. It is through their love and care that this book has been possible. Their contributions have touched every phase of this project.

John and Eleanor Ayer of Jende-Hagan Bookcorp, along with their staff have put in countless hours to produce this book.

Finally, I am indebted to my very fine research assistant, Christine Zeiler, who has spent untold hours tracking down bits and pieces of information. Her travels have taken her all over Denver to libraries, archives, book stores, and newspapers; she has painstakingly proofed and typed the manuscript; and she has provided a courier service to get things to me in Dallas.

To each and every one, I am deeply indebted for the time and trouble they went to. It is their care and thoughtfulness that has made this book what it is.

My sincere thanks.

D.J.E.

INTRODUCTION

Several years ago, while working on another project, I had cause to go to the Denver Mint to get some information. The Superintendent, Mrs. Higby, was very gracious, answered my questions, showed me the materials that I sought, and then turned me over to Lynn Heinz who took me on a personal tour of the building. I had been through the Mint as a child and as an adult; but as Mr. Heinz guided me through the plant and talked about each phase of the operation, I became overwhelmed with what a truly important institution this was and that it touched my life daily. I, for one, take coins, coinage, and money for granted; and there I was in the heart of the money factory of the United States, watching coins being stamped out by the thousands; coins that would make their way around this country and some around the world.

The idea of writing a book about the Denver Mint occurred to me then, but it was to be several years before I could begin work on it. As I began this project, I had a rough idea of what I wanted to cover. I had two primary objectives: 1) to tell the story of the Denver Mint, and 2) to provide a guide to the Mint today.

I have done no original research; several other people have and have written very fine works about various aspects of the founding of a frontier town, the first mint—Clark, Gruber & Co., and the growth and development of both Denver and the Mint.

I have attempted to gather from their works the story that is written here. I am deeply indebeted to these individuals, and their works are listed in the Reference Section in the back.

Since I am not attempting to write a scholarly work, I have chosen not to footnote. When a long quote from a source is made in this text, it appears in double quotations marks and a reference is cited.

My aim is to tell a story; the true story of a frontier town and one of its first institutions, because the story of Denver and the story of the Denver Mint are very closely interwoven.

◄——

Copyright © 1983 by David J. Eitemiller. All rights reserved. This book, or any parts thereof, may not be reproduced in any manner whatsoever without the written permission of Jende-Hagan Corporation: 541 Oak Street, P.O. Box 177; Frederick, Colorado 80530

A PLATTE 'N PRESS BOOK
Published and Distributed by Jende-Hagan Book Corporation

International Standard Book Number: 0-939650-36-3
Library of Congress Catalog Card Number: 83-81354

FOREWORD

NORA HUSSEY, SUPERINTENDENT
THE DENVER MINT

OFFICE OF
SUPERINTENDENT

THE DEPARTMENT OF THE TREASURY
UNITED STATES MINT
DENVER. COLO.   80204

All of us at the Denver Mint appreciate Mr. Eitemiller's
writing and publishing the history of the Denver Mint. This
lovely building is a historic landmark in Colorado. We are
making continuous efforts to preserve its original beauty to
share with the almost 1/2 million visitors who come here
every year. Looking to the future, we are planning an extensive
expansion and improvement project which will preserve the original
building and still enable us to efficiently meet future demands
for U.S. coins.

Nora W. Hussey

Nora W. Hussey
Superintendent

TABLE OF CONTENTS

I

THE LURE OF GOLD

As civilization developed, man found it necessary to establish some method of exchange — goods for goods or goods for services. This form of barter was an awkward method; an easier one was needed. The next method of exchange used bits of precious metal; thus the first coins came into use.

The earliest known coins were made in Asia Minor about 7000 B.C. by either the Lydians or the Ionians. The Chinese, also early users of coins, shaped their coins to show what they could buy. The Greeks were the first to stamp their coins with pictures of the architecture, religion, art, and sports of their Empire.

From that early beginning, the use of coins as a means of exchange has become universal. Not only are coins useful in purchasing goods and services, but they tell a story of the people and the times in which they were used.

Since coins were made of precious metals, the country or institution minting coins had to have some form of access to those metals. It was just such a desire that brought the first white men to Colorado.

The Spanish Explorers

When the Spanish explorers first reached the New World, they were amazed by the wealth of the civilizations that they encountered. Being treated as gods, these men used their wiles to steal as much gold as they could for the glory of king and country.

While in Mexico, these explorers heard of cities to the north that had far greater wealth — cities of unimaginable wealth where the streets were paved with gold.

The lure of that wealth brought the first Spanish expedition to the area that is now New Mexico and Southern Colorado. In 1540, Francisco Vasques de Coronado led an exploration party seeking the riches of the Seven Cities of Gold — the legendary El Dorado. The expedition was a long, difficult one that ended in failure, for there was no El Dorado.

Gold Rush to California

Gold was discovered in California in 1849, and it was that event that later led to the Rush to the Rockies. In 1850, Lewis Ralston, leading a party of gold seekers to California, found 'color' (tracings of gold) at the mouth of Cherry Creek. Rather than staying, the Ralston expedition continued on its way seeking the already-proven rich country of the Pacific coast.

During the next eight years other men found tracings of gold, too. Each time gold dust was found and the news reported back to the States, new rumors spread about wealth to be found in the Pike's Peak region (Pike's Peak being the most identifiable landmark of the area).

Beginning of a Settlement

Trappers, traders, and Indians roamed the plains and mountains freely, when in 1857 one Kentucky trapper and trader, John Simpson Smith, along with his Indian wife, Wappola, and their son Jack, erected their teepee and put a picket fence around it on the south side of Cherry Creek where it empties into the Platte River. This was the first residence on the site that was to become Denver.

Earlier parties had camped on this site but only for brief periods of time. Two accounts describe the Platte River as being very wide, about 300 feet, and difficult to cross, with a depth of 12 feet in spots.

Gold Fever Strikes

Stories of early gold-finds spread; but as news traveled very slowly, it was not until 1858 that things began to happen. That spring, William Green Russell, with his two brothers, led a party from Georgia to seek gold in the Rockies. They were soon joined by a second party from Oklahoma. With 14 wagons, 32 yoke of cattle, and about 20 ponies, the two parties traveled to the Rockies.

William Russell found the first gold in the woods along Cherry Creek on July 9th, in the area near John Smith's teepee.

A third party had set out from Lawrence, Kansas. They explored the area around Colorado Springs (actually near Pike's Peak), but quickly became discouraged with the area. When news of the Russell finds reached them, they headed north, arriving at the tiny settlement on Cherry Creek in early September.

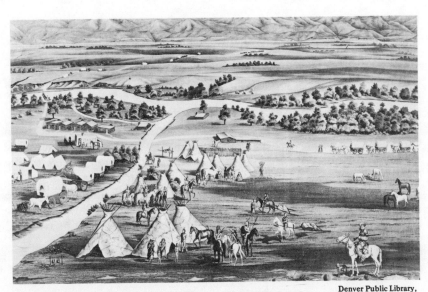

Denver, 1859 lithograph by Collier and Cleaveland Denver Public Library,
Western History Department

Other pioneers had begun to settle around the area where John Smith and his family had settled. This site at the South Platte River was on the trail between the Arkansas River and New Mexico in the south and Fort Laramie, Wyoming, in the north.

Charlie Nichols, a member of the Lawrence party, perceived the potential value of this site as a good location for a town; so he laid claim to the land north of Cherry Creek and plotted a town which he named St. Charles.

Then the settlers on the south side of the Creek got busy and on the evening of October 30th, 180 men held a meeting to lay out their own town which they called Auraria, named after the three Russell brothers' home town, Auraria, Georgia. That town had been named by John C. Calhoun during the Georgia Gold Rush of 1833, 'auraria' being a Latin adjective for gold or golden.

Caravans of men were arriving in the new settlement when in November, General William Larimer, leading a combined party of men from Leacompton and Leavenworth, Kansas, rode into town. Town fever was running about as rampant as gold fever and Larimer got it too. But to his dismay, the two best sites had already been claimed. However, Charlie Nichols and his party had departed, returning to their homes in Kansas, planning to come back to their new town the following Spring.

3

Larimer made his move. In the dead of night, he waded across the icy waters of Cherry Creek and laid claim to the deserted Nichols' claim.

As a clever politician, Larimer named his town 'Denver' in honor of James William Denver, Governor of the Kansas Territory (in 1858, the Kansas Territory stretched to the Rockies).

There was one fatal flaw in Larimer's plan. James Denver **had** been Governor when the expedition set out, but he had resigned his office while they were traveling West. The Governor resigned due to the slave/free issue raging in the Kansas Territory at that time.

The new settlers hurriedly built any kind of shelter that they could to protect themselves from the impending winter. By Christmas, the population of these two towns had reached 300. Auraria boasted 50 cabins, while Denver had only 25.

Gold is Found

The first finds of gold occurred along the Platte, but it was just gold dust that had washed down from the mountains. A group of men from the various parties set off to find the mother lode in the mountains.

One lone gold seeker, George Jackson, found a nugget in Chicago Creek, a tributary of Clear Creek (on the site of Idaho Springs); but he was out of supplies and winter was setting in, so he covered his claim and returned to the prairies to winter in the new settlement of Golden. He kept his new find a secret for a time but later found a party to join him in working the area.

Gold Fever Spreads

The border towns (towns on the border of the States and the Western territories) were responsible for fanning the flames of gold fever. When news of a new find reached the border towns, enterprising newspapers eagerly printed the stories, enlarging them. The news spread East, growing as it went. August 26, 1858, the **Kansas City Journal of Commerce** reported one such story with the banner headline, "The New El Dorado!!! Gold in Kansas!! The Pike's Peak Mines!".

A westward migration meant prosperity for those towns, because eager gold seekers would have to travel through them to get to the gold fields. Those towns took adequate measures to prepare for the hoards going West by stocking their shelves and advertising.

Their ploy worked. As gold fever spread, would-be fortune seekers in the East started West. Some came to seek fortunes; others prepared to seek their fortunes providing the goods and services that the miners would need.

Clark, Gruber & Co. Founded

One enterprising trio were the brothers Austin and Milton Clark from Ohio, and Emanuel Henry Gruber from Maryland. In the spring of 1858, these men formed a partnership to open a bank in Leavenworth, Kansas. Their bank would purchase gold dust using coined money and then ship the dust to the mints in the East. Their firm was named Clark, Gruber & Co.

Already on the Western Front

By December of 1858, the stage was set and the players in place— gold had been found in the Rocky Mountains; a settlement had begun at the confluence of the Platte River and Cherry Creek; enterprising men had joined forces to provide for the miners' needs; and news of 'gold' was spreading like wildfire.

Austin M. Clark
1824-1877

Milton E. Clark
1827-1904

Emanuel H. Gruber
1833-Date Undetermined

All photographs Denver Public Library Western History Department

RUSH TO THE ROCKIES

In the East, the Panic of 1855 caused businesses to close, banks to foreclose on homes and farms, savings to be wiped out, and unemployment to run high. News of gold in the 'Pike's Peak Region' offered hope to those affected by economic hardships.

In 1859, a long line of fortune seekers set out for the golden West. They traveled on horseback, in wagons of varying shapes and sizes, on foot, and some even pushed wheelbarrows filled with their meager belongings. They came from all States of the Union to trudge over 500 miles across the Great American Desert.

Two trails were used; one along the Platte River, and a second along the Arkansas River. A new trail was blazed across central Kansas leading directly to Auraria/Denver—The Smoky Hill Trail.

Ten years after the fabled Forty-niners headed west to California, men once again set out on a great westward migration in search of easy wealth. Rush to the Rockies was on. Wagons and carts bore the inscription 'Pike's Peak or Bust'. And Auraria/Denver, at the western end of the long trek, boomed.

Gold Finds in the Mountains

George Jackson with his new partners returned to his claim on Chicago Creek in March. By May, their supplies were short; but they were flush with new gold. Jackson went to Denver to purchase supplies but could not hide his new-found wealth. He attracted such attention that he was followed back to the hills. A new rush was on from Auraria/Denver to the mountains.

Miners quickly spread further up Clear Creek to seek out their own finds. A major find was made in May by John Gregory from Georgia in a gulch now bearing his name (down from Central City). He found the first outcropping of a rich lode in a vein of gold-bearing quartz. By the end of the summer, 150,000 men were working claims along Clear Creek. Gregory was completely stunned by his access to great wealth; he was heard to keep muttering, "My wife will be a lady and my children educated."

Money in a Mining Camp

The gold seekers had very little in coined money and practically

Larimer Street, 1859

Denver Public Library Western History Department

no paper money. As in many mining camps, gold dust became the major medium of exchange. Men carried pouches to hold their dust, often mixed with brass fillings to 'stretch' its value; and merchants had scales to weigh the dust for purchases.

Clark, Gruber & Co. became one of the heaviest purchasers of gold dust, paying $12 to $16 an ounce for the precious metal. They paid in gold coins and then shipped the dust east to be minted. But shipping was very slow and very expensive—to ship the dust from Auraria/Denver to the States could take anywhere from three weeks to three months with extensive freight charges. It cost 5% of the value of the goods shipped, with an additional 5% of the value of the goods as an insurance against loss in transit. The only forms of transportation were stagecoach or ox cart. Often there was as much as $300,000 in transit. Gruber felt that was too long a period of time to have so much money out of hand and that the freight charges were too high, so he conceived the idea of coining the gold in Denver itself.

Plans for a Mint

Gruber spoke to his partner Austin Clark about his idea. Clark, a lawyer, spent several days researching the laws but could find no law prohibiting the coining of money by a private citizen, provided that the coin was of full weight. To make sure that this was the case, Gruber consulted with two other attorneys. Both these men agreed with the finds of Clark. The firm of Clark, Gruber & Co. then proceeded to order the needed machinery.

Two Small Towns—Side by Side

Auraria/Denver had a population of 2,000 by the end of 1859. The following year, the population swelled to 4,500.

1860

The rival communities of Auraria and Denver were growing and developing as a single unit with a compatible street system, but there was a fierce rivalry between the two towns. The feelings were so intense that William Byers, founder of the **Rocky Mountain News**, built his newspaper office on stilts in Cherry Creek between Auraria and Denver. He hoped that by locating his headquarters in a neutral zone he could sell his papers to both camps.

The men of both Auraria and Denver feared competition from the rival community of Golden at the foot of the mountains. It was this fear that helped them to settle their differences and join the two towns into one. This union was effected: the name 'Denver City' was chosen; and on the evening of April 6, 1860, a torchlight parade was held on the newly completed Larimer Street Bridge over the Platte River to celebrate.

The Collier Collection, First Federal Savings Bank of Colorado

Clark, Gruber & Co., Bank & Mint, c. 1860

III

GOLD DUST TO COINS

Clark, Gruber had purchased lots on the northwest corner of McGaa and 'G' Streets (now 16th and Market), where they erected a two-story brick building with a stone basement. This was a very fine building for a town where many of the initial buildings were crude and temporary ones built of logs and canvas with dirt floors. Only 20 of the 400 odd buildings were made of brick. The machinery for their operation arrived in Denver April 2; and by July 5, they were ready to begin operations.

The Mint Opens

William Byers, in the **Rocky Mountain News** on July 25, 1860, reported receiving a note from the firm, which read:

"We shall be pleased to have you visit our coining room and witness the process of stamping our first coin from Pike's Peak gold.

Very Respectfully,
Clark, Gruber & Co.''

Byers attended and wrote the following account:

"In compliance with which invitation, we forthwith repaired to the elegant banking house of the above firm on the corner of McGaa (Market) and F streets*, and were admitted to their coining room in the basement, where we found preparations almost complete for the issue of Pike's Peak coin. A hundred 'blanks' had been prepared, weight and fineness tested and last manipulations gone through with, prior to their passage through the stamping press. The little engine that drives the machinery was fired up, belts adjusted, and between three and four o'clock the machinery was put in motion and 'mint drops,' of the value of $10 each, began dropping into a tin pail with the most musical 'clink.' About a thousand dollars were turned out, at the rate of fifteen or twenty coins a minute, which was deemed satisfactory for the first experiment.

The coins—of which none but ten dollar pieces are yet coined—are seventeen grains heavier than the U.S. coin of the same denomination.

On the face is a representation of the peak, its base surrounded by a forest of timber, and 'Pike's Peak Gold' encircling the summit. Immediately under its base is the word 'Denver,' and beneath it 'Ten D.' On the reverse is the American Eagle, encircled by the name of the firm 'Clark, Gruber & Co.' and beneath it the date, '1860.'

The coin has a little of the roughness peculiar to newness, but is upon the whole, very creditable in appearance, a vast improvement over 'dust' as a circulating medium."

*This should actually be 'G' Street—Byers evidently didn't know his way about the new town too well.

Advertisements for the firm appeared in the **Rocky Mountain News** and the **Rocky Mountain Herald** that August. Later that month, the **News** had the following account of the firm's development:

"Our Mint—Clark, Gruber & Co., melted and coined last week about $18,000 in $10, $5, and $2.50 pieces.

ADVERTISEMENTS.

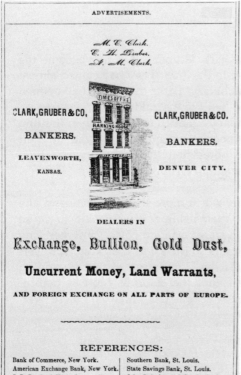

M. E. Clark.
E. H. Limber.
A. M. Clark.

CLARK, GRUBER & CO,

BANKERS,

LEAVENWORTH,
KANSAS.

CLARK, GRUBER & CO.

BANKERS,

DENVER CITY.

DEALERS IN

Exchange, Bullion, Gold Dust,

Uncurrent Money, Land Warrants,

AND FOREIGN EXCHANGE ON ALL PARTS OF EUROPE.

REFERENCES:

Bank of Commerce, New York.	Southern Bank, St. Louis.
American Exchange Bank, New York.	State Savings Bank, St. Louis.
J. S. Cronise & Howard, "	John J. Anderson & Co., St. Louis.
Work, McCouch & Co., Philadelphia.	Allen, Copp & Nesbit, "
Bullitt & Fairthorne, "	Gilmore, Dunlap & Co., Cincinnati.

Advertisement from the
**LEAVENWORTH CITY DIRECTORY AND
BUSINESS MIRROR, 1860-1861**
Courtesy of the Kansas Historical Society

As specimens of coinage these pieces are far superior to any of the private mint drops issued in San Francisco, and are nearly as perfect as the regular United States mint issues. The faces of the $5's and $2.50's are a good imitation of the government coinage — head of the Goddess of Liberty, surrounded with thirteen stars, with the name of 'Clark, Gruber & Co.' occupying the head tiara. The reverse of the coins is occupied, of course with 'our noble bird' encircled by the words, 'Pike's Peak Gold, Denver, 2½D.' Altogether it is a creditable piece of work, and we hope to see hosts of it in circulation before the snow flies. The fineness of this coin is 828½; and the excess of weight over U.S. coin is twenty-three grs. in a ten dollar piece. The value in gold is the same as government coin of like denomination, with an additional value in silver alloy equal to near one per cent. Deduct the cost of coining at the U.S. Mint, about one-half per cent, and the actual worth of Clark, Gruber & Co.'s coin is one-half per cent more than any other coinage.''

Gold Coins and Paper Money

By October, the coins issued by Clark, Gruber & Co. had become the principle medium of exchange used in the area. They had coined almost $120,000 using their basement machinery. Later that year they opened a branch bank at Central City in the heart of the gold fields.

In addition to their coined money, Clark, Gruber began issuing demand notes, a form of paper money, redeemable in gold at their Denver house. The first demand notes that they issued were steel-engraved $5 notes which were marked 'Territory of Jefferson, Denver, 1860.'

Clark, Gruber coins were actually worth more than U.S. coins of like issue. The firm did that to insure their value and were able to do so because of the money they saved in transportation costs. However, one of the drawbacks of making their coins so pure was that they were soft and wore easily. The following year the firm corrected that by adding alloys to strengthen the coins, but kept the value as high as before. The only difference in appearance was that the first coins were 'yellower' than those with alloys added.

The View of an Eastern Visitor

Upon visiting the firm during his trip to the West, Horace Greeley cabled his paper in New York, "Colorado is essentially a gold state. In the banking establishment of Clark, Gruber & Co., I saw immense quantities of gold bars lying on their counters. Come West."

Library, State Historical Society of Colorado

Library, State Historical Society of Colorado

Five Dollar Demand Note issued in 1861, with the likeness of Governor Gilpin

1861

The fledgling Denver City was developing as a supply center and a stopping place between the States and the mountain gold fields. Besides the supply stores, the chief business was housing and entertaining men in transit. Gambling halls and saloons abounded.

Denver was just a small, walking town—about ¾ of a mile in radius—when the Territory of Colorado was established, February 28, 1861. Just six short weeks before the first shots of the Civil War were fired, President Lincoln appointed William Gilpin First Territorial Governor.

Clark, Gruber continued their minting and banking work. New dies were cast, and the demand notes were changed to include the likeness of Governor Gilpin in the lower right-hand corner, and the name 'Colorado' appeared on the notes.

With the advent of the Civil War, paper money stabilized so the demand for gold coins dropped. Clark, Gruber then processed the gold

The coins issued by Clark, Gruber & Co.,   1860-61

13

dust into ingots stamped with their firm's emblem and giving the weight in ounces and the cash value. The ingots were accepted world-wide at their stamped value; some of them finding their way to Europe and Australia.

Gilpin arrived in Denver in May; and as a former military man, he quickly organized a territorial militia to protect the gold fields against the threat of a Confederate States' attack.

Political activities picked up with Gilpin's arrival. The Republican Party had its first convention at Golden that summer and one of the resolutions adopted declared the necessity for a government mint and pledged the party support in whatever might be necessary to procure it.

Clark, Gruber actually favored this measure, possibly feeling that they were engaging in a business that bordered on the edge of legality; although they were completely respected and beyond reproach in conducting business.

Mr. Clark Goes to Washington

Austin Clark accompanied Hiram Bennet, the Territory's delegate, on his journey to Washington. There, Clark presented specimens of the firm's coins to Congress. The Secretary of the Treasury sent the coins to the U.S. Mint in Philadelphia which reported the coins to be of full weight and fineness in value.

The Attorney General issued a report to President Lincoln and later to Congress stating that no law had been violated. The Secretary of the Treasury recommended that the existing coinage laws be amended so as to prevent private coinage in the U.S.; that a branch mint be established in Denver; and that the property of Clark, Gruber & Co. along with all its equipment be purchased for this new facility.

Deliberations for the purchase continued for several months; but with the Civil War going on, these discussions were of minor importance. The city of New York, which wanted an assay office, thought the idea of a branch mint and assay office in Denver too expensive. Philadelphia, however, favored it, fearing that New York really wanted the U.S. Mint moved there.

Congress Votes to Buy Clark, Gruber & Co.

The bill to establish a government-owned mint in Denver was introduced by Hiram Bennet on December 19, 1861. It was passed by both houses and became effective on April 26, 1862. Due to the slow work by the commission that was appointed to ascertain the value of the Clark, Gruber property, and because of problems dealing with the title to the land, it was not until the following year that the Government took final possession of the building.

14

Library, Colorado Historical Society

IV

THE U.S. DENVER MINT, 1863 to 1904

The early years of the little town named Denver were very difficult ones. Calamity after calamity struck, but the town survived each blow, even though a few were very close calls.

Fire struck on April 19, 1863. Prior to that there had been a long, dry spell. The fire, aided by gusty winds, quickly spread. The fledgling city did not have a waterworks or a fire department. The fire started during the night; and by the time it was out, much of the business section had been destroyed.

Since many of the buildings were little more than clapboard shacks, this wasn't surprising. The Mint, being built of brick, survived unscathed. The merchants rebuilt, and they too used brick. Because of this fire, a city ordinance was passed requiring all buildings built in the city to be constructed with brick.

Robbery, Flood, and Indian Uprising

The following year, 1864, proved to be one of the most difficult years in the city's history. The Civil War was at its peak, the population of Denver had dropped, and the surface gold had played out. New methods were needed to extract the gold from the refractory ores.

That year, three unusual events occurred in Denver. On Saturday, February 13, at about 9:00 p.m., James D. Clarke, a young pay clerk who worked in the Mint, stole gold and treasure notes worth about $37,000. Clarke had been highly thought of; but access to large amounts of money, coupled with excursions into the seamier side of frontier life was too much for the young man.

Purchasing a horse, he made his get-away east. A gold bar weighing about 10 pounds was too awkward to carry, so he threw it away (in what is now Cheesman Park).

15

Six days later, three men, including the son of his boss, caught up with him and brought him back to Denver. Not being an experienced horseman, he had lost his horse! All but about $4,500 of his take was recovered. The gold bar had been found by two men wandering in the area. It was recovered when one of them tried to sell it after sawing it in half.

Clarke later escaped from the jail and hid about town for a few days, then headed north. He was caught a second time and returned to Denver. He was brought to trial and told to leave the Territory. He was considered little more than a juvenile delinquent. With the Civil War going on and Indian uprisings, Denver had more important things to worry about.

In the early morning of May 20, heavy rains started a flash flood that caused mild little Cherry Creek to overflow its banks, washing away buildings, and killing several persons. The **Rocky Mountain News** building which had been built on stilts in the Creek was washed away.

Then during spring and summer the Plains Indians, unhappy with the migration of the white men coming West, attacked wagon trains loaded with supplies bound for Denver, killing the drivers and cutting off the supply routes to the city. With the rest of the country at war, this problem was of little concern to the federal government.

In June, rumors of an impending Indian raid on the city caused panic. Women and children were housed overnight in non-frame buildings, the Mint being one such building. The raid never occurred, and the following year the uprisings were put down.

The Denver Mint

The government took possession of the Mint building in 1863 and immediately enlarged the building; but Congress decided that because of the hostility of the Indian tribes along the routes, coining operations would be discontinued. So from 1863 to 1906 the Denver Mint in actuality functioned as an assay office. Its activities were restricted to melting and stamping unrefined bullion brought in by miners. The bars were stamped as to the 'fineness' (amount of gold and silver contained and weighed). Also stamped on the bars was a device bearing the American eagle and around it the words "U.S. Branch Mint, Denver."

This operation continued until 1904. By 1889, the Mint, rundown and worn, was said to be the only city or government building not a credit to the city.

The Silver West

The miners working the sluice boxes in search of gold were hampered by a heavy black sand that kept getting in their way. Finally, someone thought to have it assayed. It was silver! Boom times once again hit Colorado.

The Collier Collection, First Federal Savings Bank of Colorado

The Denver U. S. Mint c. 1864, with tower and addition.

Rich deposits of silver were found in many areas of the mountains. And fortunes were made and lost in silver mining. From 1872 to 1899, dollar for dollar, Colorado produced more silver than gold. By 1900, the Denver Mint reported the values of the two precious metals mined in Colorado from 1859 to 1900 as: Gold, $250 million and Silver, $541 million. (Pure gold being valued at $20.67 per ounce, while silver was $.61 an ounce.)

Plans for a New Mint

In 1895, Congress enacted legislation providing for a new Mint in Denver; a building which was to include facilities for the coinage of gold and silver. The site at West Colfax Avenue and Cherokee Street was purchased for $60,000 on April 22, 1896; but construction did not begin until late summer of 1899. The new Mint was to be 100 x 200 feet, three stories high, and have 100 rooms.

The old Mint remained in use until 1904 when the personnel moved into the uncompleted new building. The old building was sold and used as a vegetable market. Charles Boettcher bought it in 1909 and tore it down.

After

Civic Center as it appeared 1913 to 1919.

Denver—a City Emerging

From its small beginning in 1857, Denver continued to grow. It was centrally located to the mining camps of the mountains as well as the farms and ranches of the plains. With the railroad coming into Denver from the East, it became a supply center—a break of bulk point. Mining towns flourished and faded, but Denver continued to grow.

By the turn of the century, a city was emerging. Robert Speer, Mayor of Denver for ten of the years between 1904-1918, had a vision of a fine city, with parks, parkways, shade trees, sewers, paved streets, and a Civic Center.

Speer pushed his plans, and they slowly came into being. The Denver Mint is now next to Speer's dream, the Denver Civic Center.

Denver Public Library Western History Department

View from the State Capitol 1902 to 1912.

Denver Public Library Western History Department

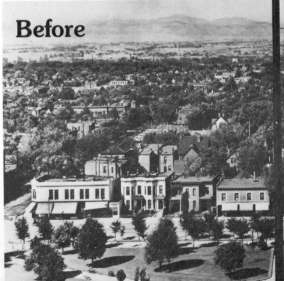

Before

V

THE NEW DENVER MINT

Although Congress made the initial appropriation for a new mint in 1895, and a site was purchased the following year, it was not until July of 1899 that the contractor, John McIntyre, received word from Washington authorizing him to proceed with construction. One hundred granite cutters were employed to dress the stone for the building, and about 30 builders were employed to do the construction work. An additional 20 men were put to work at the quarries.

The Building

The stone facing of the building is Colorado granite, from quarries in Loveland. The Arkins granite above that was procured in Maine, since large slabs were required. Tennessee marble forms the window trimmings, and Vermont marble was used on the interior finish.

The decoration of the main corridor on the first floor, mezzanine floor, and the second floor were completed under the direction of John Gibson, a member of an old Philadelphia firm. The three mural paintings in the area above the cornice inside the main vestibule are the work of Vincent Aderente, who worked under the supervision of the celebrated mural artist Edwin Howland Blashfield of New York City. The paintings represent Commerce, Mining, and Manufacturing.

The Great Seal of the United States, in the form of a large metal casting, was placed in the center of the vestibule floor.

The framework of the building is steel. Viewed from the street, the Mint gives the impression of being two stories high; but there are actually five floors.

The original appropriation for the building stated that costs were not to exceed $500,000, but this amount proved to be insufficient and was increased to over $800,000.

During construction numerous delays occurred. The Mint, however, was completed in about four years. The offices of the old Mint were moved into the new building in 1904.

The New Mint under construction c. 1901 Library, State Historical Society of Colorado

Coinage

Coins were not minted at the new facility until 1906 because the new machinery to be used at the Mint was first sent to the St. Louis Exposition of 1904 for display.

Finally in 1906, gold coins were again minted in Denver, and for the first time, silver coins. During that first year, 167 million coins were produced. There were $20 gold pieces called double eagles, $10 gold pieces called eagles, $5 gold pieces called half eagles, and assorted denominations in silver.

In 1909, the new Lincoln penny was added to the coins minted in Denver; and in 1911, $2.50 gold pieces, called quarter eagles, were minted.

Gold denominations continued until March 6, 1933 when Franklin Roosevelt signed the bill that banned the minting of gold coins. The United States discontinued using gold coins for commerce, and the gold was converted to bullion and stored in the vaults.

The Second Mint Robbery

The Mint was robbed a second time in 1920. This robbery was similar to the first in that it was committed by an employee. During one process in the minting of gold coins, anodes of pure gold measuring seven inches by three inches by one inch were produced. These anodes were so valuable that the guards on the doors were told to keep special watch out for possible theft.

21

The New Denver Mint, c. 1906   Denver Public Library Western History Department

One employee, Orville Harrington, was able to take several of the anodes without being detected. Harrington, who lived in South Denver, managed to smuggle $80,000 worth of gold anodes out of the Mint before being detected. He would bury the gold under his back walk, intending later to pass it off as gold that he had mined from his mine in Victor.

Rowland Goddard, Supervisor of the U.S. Secret Service in Denver, received a tip from a fellow employee of Harrington's; so Goddard watched him. Goddard even went so far as to hide in the weeds of a vacant lot by Harrington's home, where he saw Harrington bury the gold.

Harrington was caught and arrested for the theft. All the gold was recovered. When the newspapers found out that Harrington had a wooden leg, they made a bigger story out of it. One newspaper went so far as to have an artist draw a sketch of how a wooden leg could be hollowed out for a hiding place.

Harrington, however, didn't need to be that crafty. Due to his artificial leg, he walked with a limp, which caused him to slump, allowing his coat and vest to hang loosely over his left side; and it was in the left vest pocket that he carried out the anodes.

Harrington was not as lucky as Jim Clarke in 1864. He was found guilty and sentenced to 10 years in prison, but was paroled after three and a half years.

Federal Bank Truck Raided at Mint

One of the most daring crimes in Denver's annals occurred at the Mint; however, the Mint wasn't robbed, but a Federal Reserve Bank truck parked in front. Treasury officials are quick to point out that the Mint has an excellent record of security; however, the crime has become known as the Denver Mint Robbery.

The Federal Reserve Bank of Denver (actually a branch bank of the Kansas City Federal Reserve Bank at that time) had offices in the Interstate Trust Building at 16th and Lawrence Streets. However, the vaults in that office were not adequate to store large amounts of currency or coins, so the excess was stored at the Mint. This arrangement was unsatisfactory to all concerned.

Plans had been made to transfer $200,000 (all in new $5 bills) from the Mint to the bank. On the morning of December 18, 1922, J. E. Olson, cashier of the bank, had William Havenor drive him to the Mint in the bank pick-up truck to get the money. The truck had a wire mesh over a framework and doors that could be locked on the back. Guard C. T. Linton accompanied them.

It was a bitter cold day in Denver with a light snow on the ground, but Colfax Avenue in front of the Mint was clear and dry.

At about 10:40 a.m., the truck pulled up in front of the Mint. R. J. Grant, Superintendent of the Mint, already alerted by telephone, was ready at the front door with two guards and two packages of bills. Each package held $100,000.

The three men got out of the truck. Linton opened up the rear doors of the truck as two guards came down from the Mint, put the packages inside, then returned to the Mint.

Just as they were leaving, a big black Buick touring car drove along side the bank truck. There was a shout of, "Hands up," as three men leaped from the car. Olson hit the sidewalk; Havenor dove under the truck, sustaining multiple cuts and bruises; while Linton turned in response to the shout, and was hit with a charge of buck shot in the abdomen. One of the men removed the two packages of notes, while the other two stood guard behind telephone poles on the far side of the street. A bloody skirmish lasting but a few minutes ensued. In a rain of bullets, windows all around were shattered, the stone about the door was hit, and a couple of the bandits were apparently wounded.

On a signal from the driver, the bandits leaped into the car and headed east on Colfax, almost hitting a light truck at Bannock Street, causing it to jump the curb and hit a water hydrant.

23

The bandits were then pursued by a motorist in the area, but he lost sight of them after they turned the corner at Pearl Street and disappeared.

Linton, the bank guard, died of the wounds he received from the shotgun blast.

An exhaustive search for the criminals began, but not until 18 days later was the battered car found in a rented garage at 1631 Gilpin Street. In the front seat was the frozen body of one of the men who died from a gunshot wound. He was identified as Nicholas Trainor, alias, J. S. Sloane, a member of the Harold Burns gang.

Sloane was buried at public expense with a funeral attended by a multitide of women, one of whom thought that he might be her husband who had recently disappeared.

Part of the money, $80,000, was recovered in St. Paul; but no one was ever charged with the crime. In 1925, officials announced that they had solved the crime, but never released any details. In 1934, Denver Police Chief A. T. Clark said that the five men and two women responsible for the robbery were either dead or serving time in prison for other crimes.

When pieces of the puzzle were fitted together, this drawing appeared in the newspaper depicting the supposed events on the day of the robbery (1) At 8 a.m., the gang met at the Altahama (an apartment house). (2) About 9 a.m., the four male members of the gang left the apartment in a stolen car. (3) Between noon and 1 p.m., voices of members of the gang were heard in the apartment. It is assumed they were dividing the money before leaving Denver. (4) Two days after the robbery, Mrs. Sloane, widow of the dead robber, and Mr. and Mrs. Harold Burns left the apartment about 3 p.m. carrying suitcases. (5) The photo of the Altahama shows the windows (circle and arrow) of the apartment where the gang lived.

Denver Public Library Western History Department

The Denver Mint, c. 1935

Bullion Transfer

The center portion of the Mint was entirely remade in 1936 into a building to safeguard the gold bullion. In the fall of 1934, the Government had transferred two and one-half billion dollars worth of bullion from San Francisco to Denver for greater security offered by an inland location. Later, another billion was transferred. In today's market that would be about 100 billion dollars worth of gold bullion.

The gold was shipped by parcel post on 75 railroad mail cars, divided into 25 trains. At the Denver depot, the gold bricks were transferred onto mail trucks. The trucks were then escorted to the Mint by police cars in front and in back using sirens. This made quite an arrival.

Pennies and Nickels Go to War

During World War II, both copper and nickel were needed for the war effort. Since copper was needed for cannon shells, a war-time penny was issued in 1943 without any copper. Instead, it was minted from zinc-coated steel. About 1,093 million of the pennies were minted at all three mints that year.

A wartime nickel was issued in October, 1942. The coins were made without nickel. They, too, were struck by all three Mints until 1945.

After the war, the process of making shells from pennies was reversed. The Mint received shipments of cartridge cases from 50-caliber machine-gun bullets to melt down and mint pennies. Fifteen tons of shells were used each month to make over 30 million pennies.

The Denver Mint as viewed from Civic Center as construction begins on the City & County Building, 1924

Additions to the Building

An addition to the building in 1936 covers an area of approximately 6,000 square feet and consists of a basement and two stories. The old building was remodeled to some extent in connection with the expansion and rearrangement of operating departments. Improvements in structure and equipment include modern protective devices, added vault facilities, new machinery and an electrical precipitator system.

In 1945, another major addition was added to accommodate large-scale rolling equipment patterned after modern brass mill operations to handle an ingot weighing 415 pounds (bronze). Not until 1955 was an iron fence put around the outside.

A third addition was made in 1964, as more space was needed.

Additions to the Mint, 1956

Denver Public Library Western History Department

Commission on Community Relations, City and County of Denver.
Tom Masamori, Photographer

Kimpo Hanaya, creator of this unique coin art, stands before his dazzling display in the Oriental Gallery of the Denver Art Museum.

This unique and rare coin collection exhibit was displayed at the Denver Art Museum, then at the Mint and is now on display at the new Denver Police Building. The abstract pattern of 7,177 Oriental Coins was formally presented to the people of Denver on November 19, 1975. The display weighs over 800 pounds. Some of these ancient coins are over a thousand years old, and many are extremely rare, even priceless in Japan.

Denver and Colorado Convention and Visitors Bureau

Queen City of the Plains

From a small, clapboard, dusty frontier boom town, Denver has grown into a thriving metropolis. Today, the metropolitan area is close to two million in population; and the city is still experiencing a boom.

As a frontier town, Denver grew because it became a supply center. Later, the city became famous for its dry, clear air and was a reputed spa area for persons with respiratory diseases, particularly the dreaded tuberculosis. Many persons who had this disease and were expected to die were sent to Denver. They were carried off trains on stretchers and put in sanitariums with open air wards and rooms. Some of them made complete recoveries then stayed to make their homes here and build this major city.

Over the years, Denver became a government town with many departments of the Federal government having offices in or near the Denver area. At one time, Denver was second only to Washington, D.C., as a federal center.

Today, Denver is one of the major centers of the airline world with a major air terminal. Many national industries also have offices in the area. As a tourist center, Denver plays host to thousands of people a year who come to Colorado for winter and summer sports' recreation or conventions.

VI

THE DENVER MINT TODAY

The United States Mint is still housed in the building that was built at the turn of the century. With additions, renovations, and remodeling, it is still producing a major portion of the coins used daily by millions of Americans.

During the 1970s, there was a movement to build a new facility at a different location; but after six years of planning, controversy, expenditures, and frustrations, those plans were dropped.

Coinage Today

Gone are the gold pieces and the silver coins. Today the Mint produces cupro-nickel coins because the value of silver has gone up so high. The demand for coins has also increased, and the Mint produces over seven billion coins a year.

The Process of Making a Coin

The process of making a coin has changed drastically from the days when Clark, Gruber & Co. stamped coins in their shop at 16th and Market Streets. Today there are nine major steps in that process.

Whereas, the Mint previously took refined ingots and pressed them into rolls, that part of the operation is now contracted out.

Following is the step by step process used in the Denver Mint today to make a coin.

1   Materials are shipped to the Denver Mint from private manufacturers.

2   The rolls of metal are set into straightening reels.

3   From the straightening reel (at right of photo), the roll is fed into the punch press, which punches out round pieces of metal about the size of the coin that it is to become. These round pieces are called blanks or planchets.

4　These boxes contain metal scraps from the blank presses. After the blanks are punched out, metal clips left over are melted and remade into rolls.

5   The blanks are then put into furnaces to be softened (annealing). The furnaces are heated to approximately 1400 degrees Fahrenheit. The blanks come out of the furnaces red hot and are dropped into water to cool. They are then cleaned, polished, rinsed off with water, and dried.

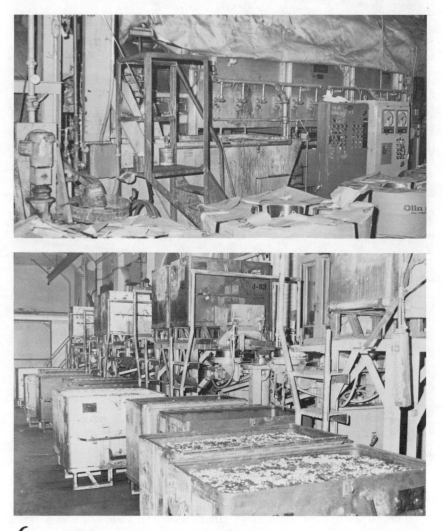

6   The blanks are fed into the Upsetting Mill Machines where they roll on their edges through the machine. They are soft enough so that when the machine presses on them it raises a rim around the blanks. The blanks are milled (upset) between disc and segment for proper diameter.

7 The Stamping presses are 225-ton Bliss presses and will stamp 550 coins per minute, both sides simultaneously, four coins at a time. The coin designs are impressed from hard steel coinage dies onto the blanks. One heavy blow stamps the coins on each side.

It takes 30 tons of pressure to stamp a penny or a dime; 60 tons of pressure for a quarter; 75 tons for a nickel; and 100 tons for a 50-cent piece.

8 Coins are screened to eliminate over or under sized coins and possible errors. Bad coins are not allowed to leave the Mint and are re-melted.

9 Coins are then counted, bagged, weighed, and stored for shipment to the Federal Reserve Banks.

When the Denver Mint first began producing coins in 1906, it produced over 167 million coins on three coin presses.

Today, there are 57 presses that operate around the clock five days a week to produce approximately 27-30 million pieces a day. That is about seven billion coins a year.

To make all these coins, the Mint employs over 375 full time employees. All employees are under Civil Service with the exception of the Superintendent and the Assayer—who are appointed by the President of the United States. Employees are thoroughly investigated before they are hired.

To insure the security of the Mint, well-trained, armed Federal Police are on duty at all times. By a thorough check in the weighing system, any discrepancy on the production floor can be traced in a short time.

The Grand Hall

This is the Grand Hall, which has been renovated recently by cleaning the beautiful marble and the artwork. It is included in the tour of the building. The green Tiffany Chandeliers are mounted in brass and just recently have been refurgished. The brass wall sconces have frosted globes. The walls and floors are of Vermont marble and are inlaid with designs. (See page 20 for the details.)

Gold Bullion

Approximately $100 billion in gold and other precious metals is stored in the vaults of the Denver Mint which has the second largest amount of gold bullion on deposit in the United States. The Depository at Fort Knox, Kentucky, has more than twice the gold stored in Denver. The rest is stored in the Depository at West Point, New York.

The Numismatic Room

Numismatic is from the Greek word for coin or money and refers to coin collecting. Coins are almost as old as recorded history, and often tell much about the civilization that used them and about the times in which they were made.

During the renovations and remodling project in 1979, the Numismatic Room was enlarged and remodeled. The sales area sells modern coins, commemorative medals, and collector's sets.

The Numismatic Room at the Denver Mint has on display many artifacts of the Denver Mint. One relic is the bronze plaque which used to grace the floor of the main entrance to the Mint. By 1969, it was so worn that it was slippery enough to pose a hazard. The Mint tried to have it repaired, but the General Services Administration didn't think that it could be done. It was replaced by a mosaic tile replica of the Great Seal of the United States.

The Sweeps Cellar

In a similar way that the gold miners in 1858 sought wealth by washing loose dirt to get gold, the Mint used to save all its dirt. Nothing was swept out of the Mint. Every speck was sacked and saved in the special sweeps cellar. Even the bath water from the employee showers was drained into a special cistern to save the residue of metallic dust which workers scrubbed off.

The sweeps contained tiny flecks of gold, silver, nickel and copper which sifted to the floor during manufacturing and cleaning. All this was sold to the highest bidder, and was a source of revenue which brought in about $25,000 a year.

Future plans for the Sweeps Cellar call for it to be changed into a movie showing area. Visitors will be able to enjoy films about the Mint and its function at the end of their tour.

Denver and Colorado Convention and Visitors Bureau

Civic Center, Historic District, 1976. Back row from left to right: The Greek Theatre, The Denver Art Museum, The University of Denver Law School, The City and County Building of Denver. Mid-row: The Denver Water Board Building (the old Public Library). Foreground: The Voorhees Memorial.

REFERENCES

Material for this book has been gathered from the sources listed below.

Single Volume Works

Arps, Louisa Ward. *Denver in Slices.* Denver: Sage Books, 1959.

Dorset, Phyllis Flanders. *The New Eldorado: The Story of Colorado's Gold and Silver Rush.* New York: The MacMillan Company, 1970.

Hafen, LeRoy R. and Ann Hafen. *The Colorado Story: A History of Your State and Mine.* Denver: The Old West Publishing Company, 1953.

Mumey, Nolie. *Clark, Gruber and Company (1860-65) A Pioneer Denver Mint: History of Their Operation and Coinage.* Denver: Aircraft Press, 1950.

Smiley, Jerome C. *History of Denver.* The Times-Sun Publishing Company, 1901.

Stone, Irving. *Men To Match My Mountains: The Story of the Opening of the Far West, 1840 to 1900.* New York: Doubleday, 1956.

Periodicals

Hafen, LeRoy R. "Currency, Coinage and Banking in Pioneer Colorado," *The Colorado Magazine,* X/3 (May, 1933), pp. 81-90.

Helmers, Dow. "The Denver Mint Robbery, 1922," *The Denver Post,* December 7, 1975, pp. 79-83.

Newspaper Articles

The Colorado Prospector: Historical Highlights from Early Day Newspapers, May, 1972, "The Denver Mint."

Other Sources

Higby, Betty, "Facts and Figures Concerning The United States Mint, Denver, Colorado," (Fact Sheet) c. 1975.

"How to Make a Penny at the Denver Mint," U.S. Government Printing Office, (Handout) 1971.

About the Author

DAVID EITEMILLER, *born and reared in Denver, is the third generation of his family to call Denver home. A graduate of East High School and the University of Colorado, with a major in Communications and Theatre, he has worked for the Elitch Theatre Company, the Denver Public Schools, and the Central City Opera House Association.*

In 1982, he received a Masters Degree in Stage Direction of Opera from Indiana University, School of Music where he was assistant to the Lighting Designer, Allen White. He served as Master Electrician for Opera Festival of the South, and Lighting Technician for the Dallas Ballet.

Currently, he is based in Dallas where he does free-lance work in directing, scenic and lighting design.

As a Colorado history buff, he has written another book on Auraria and Lower Downtown Denver and is planning a series on Denver. He is frequently in Denver on his travels.